What Do You Know About
Earth's Oceans
?

PowerKiDS
press
New York

Gillian Gosman

Published in 2014 by The Rosen Publishing Group, Inc.
29 East 21st Street, New York, NY 10010

First Edition

Editor: Jennifer Way
Book Design: Kate Laczynski
Layout Design: Colleen Bialecki

Photo Credits: Cover MCarter/Shutterstock.com; p. 5 Ozerov Alexander/Shutterstock.com; p. 6 John Woodcock/iStock Vectors/Getty Images; p. 7 Matthew Wakem/Aurora/Getty Images; p. 8 Thaiview/Shutterstock.com; pp. 8–9 Aleynikov Pavel/Shutterstock.com; p. 9 Andrea Danti/Shutterstock.com; p. 10 Jeff Rotman/The Image Bank/Getty Images; p. 11 Encyclopaedia Britannica/Universal Images Group/Getty Images; p. 12 Volodymyr Goinyk/Shutterstock.com; p. 13 Medioimages/Photodisc/Getty Images; p. 14 Dorling Kindersley/Getty Images; pp. 14–15 Dr. Robert Muntefering/The Image Bank/Getty Images; pp. 16–17 Carly Rose Hennigan/Shutterstock.com; p. 17 Mana Photo/Shutterstock.com; p. 18 AFP/Getty Images; pp. 19, 22 Martin Harvey/Peter Arnold/Getty Images; p. 20 Chris P./Shutterstock.com; pp. 20–21 iStockphoto/Thinkstock.

Library of Congress Cataloging-in-Publication Data

Gosman, Gillian.
 What do you know about earth's oceans? / by Gillian Gosman. — 1st ed.
     p. cm. — (20 questions: earth science)
 Includes index.
 ISBN 978-1-4488-9700-1 (library binding) — ISBN 978-1-4488-9858-9 (pbk.) —
 ISBN 978-1-4488-9859-6 (6-pack)
 1. Ocean—Juvenile literature. I. Title.
 GC21.5.G68 2013
 551.46—dc23
                                        2012032009

Manufactured in the United States of America

CPSIA Compliance Information: Batch #S13PK5: For Further Information contact Rosen Publishing, New York, New York at 1-800-237-9932

Contents

What Do You Know About Earth's Oceans?

The world's oceans are amazing places! They range from the freezing waters in Earth's polar regions to the warm waters of the tropics and from shallow sunlit areas to deep areas sunlight cannot reach. Earth's oceans are home to more than 250,000 known plant and animal **species**, and there are many more still to be discovered.

Earth's oceans are not just a home for plants and animals. Oceans are an important part of the water cycle. The water cycle is the process of water changing states and moving through Earth's environment. Oceans also affect Earth's weather and climate. This book will explain what Earth's oceans are and the important roles they play in our world.

There is much more to Earth's oceans than what you can see from the beach.

5

1. How much of Earth is ocean?

About 71 percent of Earth's surface is covered by ocean. Earth's oceans contain about 95 percent of Earth's water!

This map shows the world's oceans. You can see that there is really one big ocean that is broken up by the seven continents.

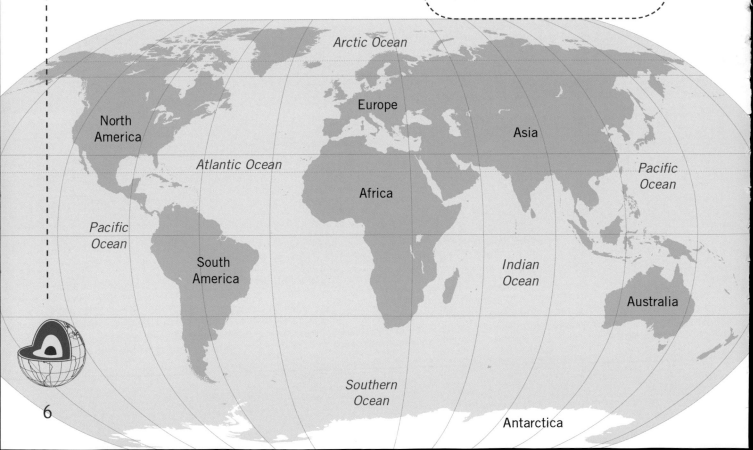

Arctic Ocean

Europe

North America

Asia

Atlantic Ocean

Pacific Ocean

Africa

Pacific Ocean

South America

Indian Ocean

Australia

Southern Ocean

Antarctica

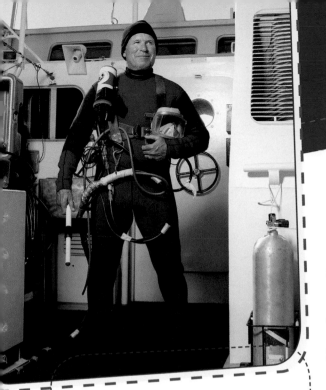

Oceanographers go out to different parts of the ocean to do their research. They sometimes put on scuba gear and go underwater to study the ocean up close.

2. How many oceans and seas are there?

The world ocean is a large, connected body of salt water. It lies between and around the planet's seven continents. The world ocean is divided into five separate oceans. They are the Pacific, Atlantic, Indian, Southern, and Arctic Oceans.

A sea is also a saltwater body. Generally, a sea is partly surrounded by land, but an ocean sits between continents.

3. What do oceanographers do?

Oceanographers are scientists who study the oceans. They study the movements of ocean water, the changes in the ocean floor, and the plants and animals that live in the oceans or depend on the oceans for food.

7

4. Why is the ocean blue?

Sunlight is made up of all colors of the rainbow but appears white. Each light color has a different wavelength, or distance between each wave. When sunlight hits ocean water, most light waves are **absorbed**. The blue light waves are **reflected**, though. This reflection of blue light waves makes the ocean look blue.

5. Why is the ocean salty?

As water travels, it picks up salt and other minerals. When this water flows into the ocean, it is deposited there, making it salty.

The sky looks blue for the same reason that the ocean looks blue.

6. How are Earth's oceans part of the water cycle?

Like other bodies of water, oceans are where water collects in the water cycle. From there the water is heated by the Sun and **evaporates** into the air and becomes **water vapor**. Water vapor **condenses** into clouds and then falls as **precipitation**. From there the water cycle begins again!

Animals that live in oceans need to live in salty water. Freshwater would kill them!

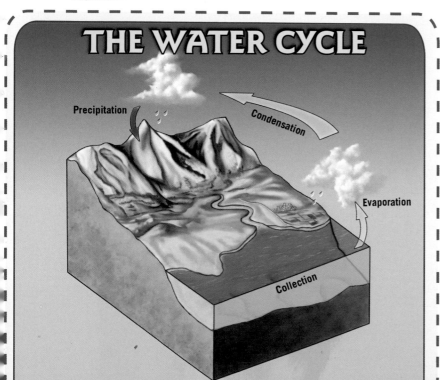

THE WATER CYCLE

Precipitation

Condensation

Evaporation

Collection

This diagram shows how water moves through the water cycle.

There are four main layers of ocean. The topmost layer is called the sunlit zone because sunlight reaches this layer. The ocean's plants grow in this layer. The next layer down is the twilight zone. This layer gets so little light that plants cannot grow there. Below this are the midnight zone and the abyss, where there is no sunlight at all.

Frogfish, like the one shown here, live in the sunlit zone.

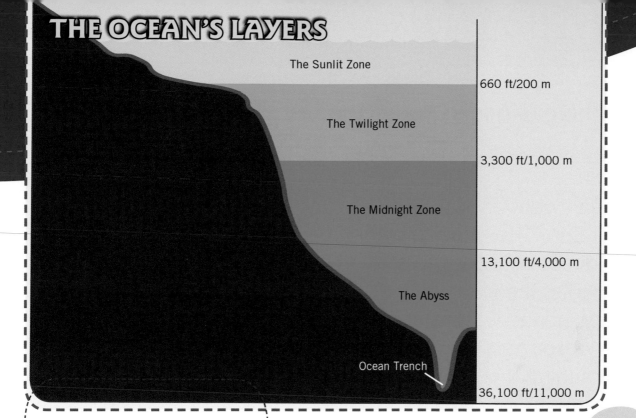

THE OCEAN'S LAYERS

The Sunlit Zone

660 ft/200 m

The Twilight Zone

3,300 ft/1,000 m

The Midnight Zone

13,100 ft/4,000 m

The Abyss

Ocean Trench

36,100 ft/11,000 m

This diagram shows the ocean's layers and the depths at which they are found.

8. Where is the ocean the deepest?

The very deepest parts of the ocean are the **trenches** along the floor. Trenches are found where **continental plates** meet. The deepest of these trenches is the Mariana Trench, in the Pacific Ocean. You would have to travel down more than 35,000 feet (10,668 m) to reach this trench's floor!

11

9. Where is ocean water the warmest?

Ocean water is warmed by the Sun. Therefore the more direct sunlight the water gets, the warmer it is. Shallow ocean water near the **equator** gets the most direct sunlight, so it has the warmest water.

In the Southern Ocean, shown here, the water deep below the surface can be as cold as 28° F (-2° C).

10. Where is ocean water the coldest?

Earth's polar regions get less direct sunlight than the areas near the equator. Therefore the coldest ocean water can be found deep below the surface of the Southern Ocean.

11. How do oceans affect climate?

The oceans absorb about 98 percent of the Sun's heat that reaches Earth's surface. The Sun's heat causes ocean water to evaporate, and this plays a role in creating weather. The movement of ocean water helps move weather around Earth. This movement follows certain paths, which create weather patterns. This is part of what gives the world different climates.

Near the equator, water in the sunlit zone can be as warm as 98° F (37° C). Shown here is the ocean near the equator in the Pacific Ocean.

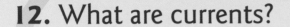

12. What are currents?

A current is the movement of water along a path. Ocean currents are caused by tides, wind, landforms, and the temperature and salt content of the water.

This map shows how ocean currents and gyres flow across Earth's surface.

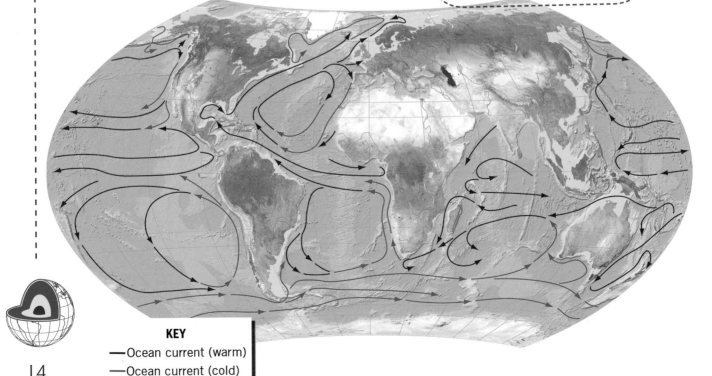

KEY
— Ocean current (warm)
— Ocean current (cold)

Hurricanes are strong storms that ocean currents play a part in forming and moving. The hurricane shown here is near the coast of Florida.

13. How do ocean currents affect climate?

Ocean currents carry water across Earth. These currents can form loose circles called **gyres** that cross entire oceans. For instance, in the Atlantic Ocean, the Gulf Stream current carries warm water northward from the equator. This warms the southeast coast of the United States. This warm water continues northeast on the North Atlantic Current to Europe. By the time it gets there, the water has cooled, however. The current then moves the water southward toward the equator on the Canaries Current. This current is carrying colder water, which cools the land along the shores in its path.

14. What causes tides?

If you stood on the beach for long enough, you would notice that the water rises and falls over many hours. This rise and fall of the water level is called the tide. It is caused by the **gravitational** pull of the Moon and, to a lesser degree, the Sun. The strength of this pull changes as Earth rotates through a day, causing high tides and low tides.

At low tide, you might see a tide pool like the one shown here. These starfish will be covered by water again at high tide.

15. What causes waves?

Most ocean waves are caused by the wind. As air moves across the surface of the water, it transmits some of its energy to the water. Strong winds make larger waves than gentle winds. Underwater earthquakes or volcanic eruptions cause large, powerful waves called **tsunamis**.

The Pacific Ocean near Hawaii is known for having lots of big waves. This makes it a great place for the sport of surfing.

Human beings have done a great deal to **pollute** the planet's oceans. In many parts of the world, garbage and other waste is dumped directly into the ocean. Oil, fertilizers, or other chemicals that get into rivers or into the ground also can be carried into the ocean through the water cycle.

This garbage washed up from the ocean onto a beach in Asia.

17. What is the Great Pacific Garbage Patch?

The oil covering this penguin harms its feathers. When it grooms itself to try to remove the oil, it swallows oil, which hurts the animal's insides.

The Great Pacific Garbage Patch shows how polluted our oceans have become. The swirling waters of the North Pacific Gyre have trapped an area of floating garbage. The Great Pacific Garbage Patch is mostly pieces of plastic bags, chemicals, and other bits of trash. Scientists have discovered that ocean animals eat this harmful garbage. They have also found that the garbage patch releases dangerous chemicals into the water.

18. What is polar ice?

Polar ice is found at both ends of Earth. This ice is made of frozen seawater. Polar ice melts and refreezes with the seasons, as the water around it warms and cools.

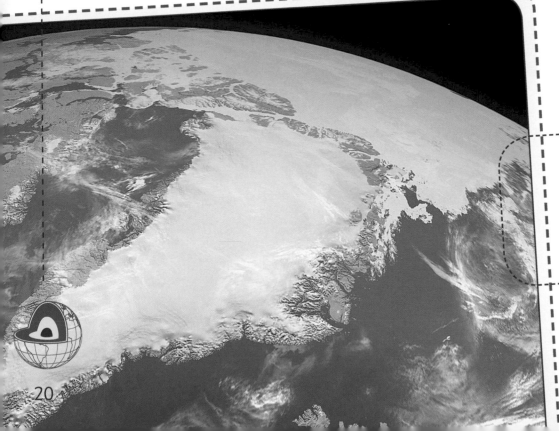

Here you can see the white polar ice on Greenland. This is part of the polar region in the North.

19. How does climate change affect polar ice and Earth's oceans?

Shrinking polar ice affects animals, too. Polar bears live on ice sheets in the North. As polar ice melts, their habitat shrinks!

Scientists have discovered that climate change has caused the polar ice caps to start melting. This is bad because the polar ice caps help control Earth's weather and climate.

Ice caps are white and reflect the Sun's heat. As an ice cap shrinks, less heat is reflected and more heat is absorbed. This can cause the ocean around the shrinking ice cap to warm and melt the ice even faster! This melting ice causes the level of ocean water to rise. Eventually this rising water level could flood cities close to ocean shores.

20. How can we protect Earth?

Everybody can help protect Earth's oceans. Many of the things we do and chemicals we use every day release pollution into Earth's air and water. This pollution can make it into our oceans and harm them. One simple way you can help Earth's oceans is to use less plastic. Plastic water bottles and grocery bags get into the ocean and can harm ocean animals and plants. Another thing you can do is to learn about conservation groups. These types of groups are a good source to learn about the different things that are being done to study and protect Earth's oceans.

Scientists study polar ice to learn about the history of Earth's climate. This helps them learn how Earth's climate has changed over time.

Glossary

absorbed (ub-SORBD) Took in and held on to something.

condenses (kun-DENTS-ez) Cools and changes from a gas to a liquid.

continental plates (kon-tuh-NEN-tul PLAYTS) The moving pieces of Earth's crust.

equator (ih-KWAY-tur) The imaginary line around Earth that separates it into two parts, northern and southern.

evaporates (ih-VA-puh-rayts) Changes from a liquid, like water, to a gas, like steam.

gravitational (gra-vuh-TAY-shnul) Having to do with gravity.

gyres (JYRZ) Circular currents on the ocean's surface.

oceanographers (oh-shuh-NAH-gruh-furz) Scientists who study the ocean.

pollute (puh-LOOT) To hurt with certain kinds of bad matter.

precipitation (preh-sih-pih-TAY-shun) Any moisture that falls from the sky. Rain and snow are precipitation.

reflected (rih-FLEKT-ed) Threw back light, heat, or sound.

species (SPEE-sheez) One kind of living thing. All people are one species.

trenches (TRENCH-ez) Deep cracks in the ocean floor.

tsunamis (soo-NAH-meez) Series of waves caused by movements in Earth's crust on the ocean floor.

water vapor (WAH-ter VAY-pur) The gaseous state of water.

Index

Websites

Due to the changing nature of Internet links, PowerKids Press has developed an online list of websites related to the subject of this book. This site is updated regularly. Please use this link to access the list:
www.powerkidslinks.com/20es/ocean/